When the Blackbird Called

Rita Traut Kabeto

Rita Traut Kabeto

When the Blackbird called
by Rita Traut Kabeto

ISBN 978-0-557-43523-4

The Vine

While strolling down the street one spring
my eyes searched out the flowers
that lined the path in softest green
and blooms of lavish colors

And coming to a garden fence
all woven through with vines
and sprouting future promises
of one and other kinds

a pair of sturdy vines reached out
and curled around my arm
and held me for a moment long
as if to beg a chance

in dance to swing me to and fro
so merrily arm-in-arm
a frisky polka, quick gambol
or waltzes, gay glissade.

To Robert Frost
on "Stopping by Woods"

The poet Robert Frost revealed,
'The woods are lovely, dark, and deep'
And with these simple little phrases
he hinted at the sacred spaces

where spruce and fir and hemlock guard,
their branches meshed as if to bar
intruders from encroaching far,
the pregnant hush of their realm

when snow lies heavy on their bows
like burdens on the human brow
and holding breath they wait and bear
the biting chill of winter's air

and guard within their hallowed midst
what neither fox nor hare can miss
for deep inside that silent soace
awaits the Self we yearn to face.

Love's Issue

*In the embrace of darkness
and the immediacy of silence
awake with wonder
lay Man*

*bewildered by the power
that had taken hostage
his yearning heart
unaware*

*and the agony that shook him
and the ecstasy that drew him
in unspeakable pain
birthed a poet.*

Hot Crow

How hot the summer heat does seep
Through feathers, black, that seize the heat
Through leath'ry socks into my feet
And through the nostrils in my beak.

Water, water everywhere
But not a drop to drink.

It's chlorinated – yukk – by rules
It's dirty, hot in stagnant pools
It's cooked to tea in people's gutters
It's spoiled by gas and oil from sputters.
There are some birdbaths here and there
With water, fresh, when people care
But cats are roaming high and low
To pounce upon unlucky crow

Water, water everywhere
Is there no drop to drink?

But ah, there is, I found at last
On shopping street and right near Max
A basin, off the ground for ease
Just right the rim for my big feet
To sit in comfort while I drink
From people's bubbling water sink.
It gushes up from deep inside
So clear and bright, a joy for eyes.

Water, water everywhere
And lots of drops to drink.

Ants

Marching and crawling
indifferent efficient
they hurry and scurry
and move in precision
removing the mortar
from concrete foundations
one grain at a time.

They work without resting
they hustle and bustle
to loosen what's fastened
and causing to crumble
what meant to be lasting
those tiny marauders
the agents of time.

White Man

He caught my eye for he was white,
so very white all over,
white his hat and white his coat
and white his penny loafers.

His pants were white and both his socks
his hands were tucked in white
and to himself he clutched a load
of laundry sheets, all white.

As he commenced to cross the street
and checked the traffic flow
his eyes met mine as I stood staring -
I was embarrassed so.

He didn't seem to mind it, though
he smiled a big broad grin
that split in half his big black face
and showed his great white teeth.

But in that instant of our meeting
our minds became as one
and I knew then what he had known
that I would know just then:

that all this whiteness set off fine
his big black face and hair
and that he looked to all the world
quite extraordinaire.

Observed on Second and Rose Streets in Walla Walla, Washington

To Robert Frost on "Mending Walls"

Some things there are that love a wall
of broad design and very tall,
boulders sharp and angular
with rugged granite surfaces.

Like social individuals
the wall must have cohesiveness
and finds it altogether smart
to hold onto the mortar's art.

The mortar thus flows through the wall
like spider's web, it covers all
it binds together rock and stone
makes nesting sites for tiny forms

of mosses, thick with luscious green,
or scraggly spread and crawling keen
with tentacles, a wooly maze
across the wall's uneven face.

And where the mortar does not reach
the charcoal stone is under siege
from creeping lichens, gray-green-white
and minerals from deep inside

that burst like flowers through the crust
to paint the boulders wine and rust
and brown and yellow, orange too
and tiny ferns are sprouting new.

Against this wondrous patchwork life
dainty sprays of graceful vines
from narrow nooks and crevices
are trailing down the precipice.

But here and there some gaps appear
the mortar dug, no moss grows there
the holes are lined with finest hair
of mouse, or mole, and even hare

and roll-up bugs and beetles all
are keeping house in that great wall
and peer at people walking past
who do not see the wall, alas.

SE Fourth and Market Streets in Portland, Oregon

2008   Someone there was who did not love the wall
        of broad design and very tall
        he made the ball tear down the wall
        and now it's only two feet small.

What Then?

When oneness sought of mind and will
of feelings, bodies, dreams
and sought by many efforts but
continues to retreat
and heart, dejected and fatigued
gives up its claim to rule
and silently retreats to nurse
its ever aching wounds -
What then?
When fun and games and whirlwind tours
no longer fill the void
when summer sunshine, birds and blooms
no longer still the mind
but something stirs and prods down deep
inside the farthest reach
and nags us days and restless nights
with deep and urgent dreams -
What then?

And what's forgotten and denied
comes haunting from the mist
that's drawn like curtain, merciful
across the great abyss
and whispers what you cannot hear
and rouses you to feel
and spurs you on with promises
of mystical appeal -
What then?
When peace gives way to restlessness
contentment turns to woe
and nothing you can do or say
can still those yearning throes
then turn inside and listen close
and find the One you sought:
the One is you, the Teacher Friend
the Teaching and the Taught.

Sidewalk

My sidewalk has a mind, its own
it doesn't like its grayish tone
so bland and hard a walking path
was never meant by nature's plan.

Compared to nature's vibrant colors
my sidewalk has a deathly pallor
and thinking how to change the matter
it came up with a plan, quite clever.

With help from rain and icy weather
it grew some cracks for all the better
to house and nourish organisms
to live and breathe in unicism.

The ones to heed the call for color
were knotweed, short with tiny flowers
and clover thick with broaden leaves
tenaciously they cling and cleave.

They weave a carpet green and dense
that comforts tired feet, so tense.
They cover all that boring pallor
throughout the year with handsome color.

Alas, the man in gardening twill
can only bide what he does will
so out come spray and garden tool
to kill the green that nature grew.

I Can Not Go to Work Today

How can I go to work today
my garden's calling me
some trees are young and need a stake
and water, pruning, feed.
Dead flowers I must pick to tease
more flowers into bloom,
and weeds galore are taking root
where veggies are to grow.

The apples, fallen to the ground,
are waiting to be made
to sauce and pies and other such,
I fear they'll go to waste.
Clematis needs a trellis pole
to climb instead of sag
and roses need my pruning touch
that flowers may not lag.

I cannot go to work today
my daughter needs a letter,
the bank needs straightening out again,
my shoes need soles of leather.
Hook and yarn have waited long
for me to work the lace,
a picture in the drafted stage
is calling me to paint.

And mending, ironing, cleaning, all
are waiting to be finished
a curse it is that all this work
refuses to diminsh.
I have to charm the feral cat
and find its catty nest
that I may catch and take it to
be neutered by the Vet.

And, oh, the words I need to free
from piles of twisted twine
that roll around within my head
all day, all day and night.
I cannot go to work today
for I must search the books
that help me clarify my thoughts
within some quiet nook.

Yet Life, that cruel enterprise
does force me off to work
that I should feed and clothe myself
and earn my cozy burg.
I'm juggling job and work and fun
and learning, need, and leisure
and last, not least, it's plausible
that I should have some pleasure.

How can I go to work today!
I need to figure out
how all these things are getting done,
that nothing's losing out.
Oh Life, you devious enterprise
you make me like so much
then take away the time to do
how you enticed me thus.

And yet - a purpose must exist
for things to be like that
for me to be inclined to do
all this and that - so much.
It seems that I'm evolving fast
into a super Being.
I thought I have eternity.
Oh Life - - - don't rush me!

Crows in Winter

Some crows sat blabbing atop a roof
To see the world from an upscale view
With heads pulled in and feathers fluffed
They braved the biting winter dusk

And watched and listened, cawed sometimes
The colder it grew, the darker the sky
A chimney emerged from a roof ridge nearby
Emitting smoke from a cozy fire.

And softly the snow began drifting down,
So wispy at first, then fluffy as down
And as it was snowing, said crow number one,
"Time to get going, my friend, lets run."

"No, stupid," said crow number two. "We'll stay.
That chimney up there is the perfect place
To warm us in comfort." And eager he leapt
To settle himself at the chimney's edge.

Urged crow number one, "let's go right now,
'ere the snow piles high and keeps us down."
"We're staying put," said crow number two,
"we'll not catch cold nor even the flue."

Felicitous crow number one gave in,
Moved close to the inner chimney rim.
"A better crow am I," said he
then pushed forth his chest to catch the heat.

The crows huddled close at the inner rim
The snow had no power, the warmth made them grin
They leaned their bodies to the rising warmth –
Daybreak discovered two cured and smoked forms.

Daisies

The little daisies in the lawn
insist on blooming still
despite the eager efforts of
the man in gardening twill.

He mowes and cuts and feeds the grass,
spreads killers out to catch
whatever doesn't look like blades
or isn't green to match.

Yet in that boring sea of grass
pop up to spite the man
the little daisies white and pure
and proudly hold their stance.

But as with people who don't like
What's different, other, new
the man reacts with his intent
of keeping lawns just green

and never realizes that
in contrast lies the beauty,
and that his lawn looks only great
when visited by daisies.

Ash Wednesday

I once was a child with natural charm,
human and hopeful joyful and sad,
instinctively trusting that omnipotent wisdom
would order all things to greatest perfection.

My body a vessel of senses that longed
to know all of life, its infinite forms
to know and to treasure the Self that I am
the bonds that connect me with people and land.

A playmate was I to wind and rain
to sunshine and thunder, snow and hail.
The sun never set on life's great adventures
its riddles and visions, heartaches and pleasures.

> *Life is a potter at the wheel of time*
> *his hands apply pressure, meanwhile*
> *a vessel is growing, evolving, refined*
> *by motion, pressure, and endless time.*

Ash Wednesday came and draped a shroud over my
innocent days. I honored the law and became a sinner,
temple of impotent Spirit. Like ancient Greeks in fear of
unpredictable Gods, I lived to appease their appetites.
To soften their wrath I implored divine mercy.

Walking the Path became a course of obstacles for sorting
sinners by degree, severity, and membership - all human
guilty and bad. For guilty was I by brotherhood long
before I acted, and bereft of ordained divinity I lost out to
foolish darkness.

But the Divine spark continued to glimmer faintly in the darkness. Sorrows and hardships turned me inward and I saw the flickering flame. It grew with continued mindfulness, nurtured by desire, until its powerful light overwhelmed the oppression of foolish darkness.

And the clay does suffer the potter's hands
his fingers caress it with wise demand
they cradle and clutch it, squeeze and release it
add life-giving water to growing perfection

Intermezzo

After the war was over
and the bomb craters had filled in
and the rubble piles had been cleared away,

and before the German economic miracle
demanded the surrender of townhouse gardens
and tore away walking spaces to make parking spaces
and replaced the star mosaic of cobbled sidewalks with square slabs

There was sunshine.
It warmed the sidewalk playground
filtered sunlight through chestnut trees and Lindens
and the quivering shadows blurred the cobbled images.
It gilded the curly heads of little children
who played with their dolls and scooters,
played catch and hopscotch and jump rope,
and the sound of their laughter adorned the still afternoon
while grown-ups withdrew to the cool seclusion
of their apartments above the shops
and rested in the twilight of dark green window shades
while life slowed down obligingly
and dozed in the tranquility
of days filled with sunshine.

Unsecured Places

Among the City's citadels
of business towers, office malls,
of human habitation squares
and tortured little nature spheres

crouching low between two giants
pencil-shaped and Borgish riot
lingers on that entium
called Keller Auditorium.

Once thought of as the City's pride
its quintessential mark of high
achievement in the arts and culture
grew insignificant in stature.

For bit by bit time had its way
with siding, windows, doors and frame.
And pigeons, crows, and gulls estranged
the entium's intended aims.

They come from all around the region
to rest, to feed, to keep allegiance
with countless others of their kind
and always leave what humans mind.

They drop it, not discriminating
on every surface, all the ledges
in front, in back, on top, outside
pigeon guards they only mind.

A first-class place it once was," sadly
said pigeon number one, and anxious
around the caked-on splatters looked
where mosses fed and fungi grew.

"My forbear used to love this place,"
said pigeon number two. "He said
that all the world did want to see
the sights from here, the mountain view.

"But now this place is just a dump
the mold and mildew grow rampant,
streaks of black and gray and yellow
make quite a mess of this old fellow.

"I'm leaving here, I've had enough.
I want to move to something smart.
That sparkling Pencil over there
is just the place I want to share.

"It's glitter is what I desire,
its cleanliness what I admire.
Gulls and crows may have the Borg,
that monstrous heap, a nature morgue."

"Wait for me," called pigeon one
and when the breeze came 'round again
the two ascended on their wings
and on their great imaginings.

Then swinging 'round that great fat Pencil,
sporting balconies and ledges,
they chose a fancy alcove inn
quite high above the downtown din.

While checking out their neighborhood
they smiled and cooed, and said, "just look!
This is the life! The view is great
and rent is free - we've got it made."

But bit by bit time has its way
with bricks and mortar, roof and frame,
and that which humans don't desire
gets washed by rain into a mire,

gives feed to mold and mildew rot,
grows lichens and bacterial spots,
invading every nook and cranny
of every building, poor or fancy.

Time is the ultimate consumer,
it harvests all that humans treasure
it calls on poor and rich alike
does not discriminate the price.

A Prayer

Don't make me go from this realm
I cannot bear to leave again
the splendor of its nature
which in perfection gently revels
and with its peaceful noise does level
the weary pilgrim's pain.

'T was you who called to me unceasing
throughout the eons, never tiring
until I head your voice
that spoke of love and mindfulness
and roused in me profound awareness
which knows all life as one.

But now that I have seen the light
you send me back to lonely night
and bitter isolation.
The world cannot accept my nature
it parcels out my earthly matter
rejects the greater Whole.

I almost wish you'd left me blind
I would not miss what stays behind
and peace would be my fate.
I know, I know, I hear you well
to live I must return again
to what I came to hate.

for perfect I am not, by far
and being of the Earth's realm
still tied in hidden ways
to earthly passions not revised
and wrongs that call for setting right
mistakes of countless lives.

To live is endless forward motion
and I will do you, Teacher, honor
by taking up the Path.
But when the awful yearning threatens
to overwhelm my courage, Master
be ready with your comfort.

Send flowers me to flood my senses
with pretty colors, fair fragrances
and ocean waves to sooth.
Send stalwart trees to guard my tears
and meadowlarks to charm my ears
and gold of sun and moon.

To vent the power of my feelings
send me the sounds and pulse of music
and laughter, innocent and hearty,
and humor, wisdom, camerad'rie.
But most important, Master Friend,
to me a kindred Spirit send
to share my Path, the joy, the sorrow
and help me bear the days of morrow.

The Village Lane
Kicklingen

Among the backyard alleys
is one that charms my mind
for it invokes uncannily
the one I knew as child.

Three strips of grassy weeds
meander down the lane
two barren tracks between them
where bicycles convey
where women walk in aprons
to shop the country store
and farmers stride with sickles
against their shoulders propped
and young and old alike
decked out in Sunday best
in shiny, polished shoes
head off to Sunday mass
and always walking right
and passing on the left
with nothing more between them
than strips of weedy grass.

The grassy, weedy fringes
commingle with the meadow
they line the drainage ditches
and creep into the pastures
they crowd into the fences
of slumping, weathered planks
that mark the start of property
and where it's bound to end.

They frame the wooden benches
beneath the Linden trees
that stand as shady invite
near open farm yard gates.

They throng around the bases
of apple trees that tease
with gnarled and mossy branches
above the sunny lane
and drop their luscious fruit
where weeds and grasses save
for mouse and insect kin
the waning summer's yield.

That all the Paths of Life
were simple as this lane
so humbly and so honestly
in purpose and in aim
connecting many elements
in diffident utility
and nothing worse than weeds
be standing in the way
of sharing Life and apples
'twixt fellow man and me.

Mums

denizens of glum
days of November
twilight December
fragrance and color
squandered in squalor
midst remnants of summer
in the graveyard realm

abode of the silent
peaceful recumbent
family members
agreeable rendered
ended is fighting
suspended the chiding
harmonious together
and pleasant at last

beneath the color
and fragrance of mums
stalwart companions
of days that are glum
the warmth of that silence
so dearly abiding
I carry with me
wherever I go

and when I recall
the season of fall
recount the splendor
the dusk and the squall
I gladly remember
the love thus engendered
on days that were glum
by the fragrance of Mums.

Childish Quest

Some flies are circling round and round
the fixture on my ceiling
back and forth in zigzag rhythm
never holding steady
this way that, abruptly changing
course and tiny minds
why don't they stop and rest themselves
I want to count their kind.

My tears have dried, I'm on my bed
where Mother sent me, angry
when she found out that I had spent
more money than she granted.
But it's my birthday, I protested,
but that was useless chatter
and Mother sent me to my room
to think on this grave matter

The windows open to the breeze
on this spring afternoon
the town abuzz down on the street
how dull to be indoors.
There's nothing I can do but stare
and count the circling flies
their zigzags do confound me so
and over again I start.

But ere I have a chance at four
they've rearranged themselves.
Over and over again I start
but finally I'm sure
that there are seven flies in flight
around the ceiling fixture
but never did I learn that time
their landing skill, so expert.

A Daughter's Plea

Why don't you like me, Mother? Why?
That question haunts me daily.
I should have asked when you could answer
instead of waiting lately.

Still, I know what you'd have answered
'What makes you say such things?'
And with much logical conviction
'I treat you all the same.'

Your forehead would be wrinkled up
in fretful irritation
your raised eyebrows would deny
my query's implication.

And growing then defensive, you
would make me feel so bad
for failing, once again, to make
you hear what I have said.

And once again I cannot get
what I so badly need
a touch from you, a holding tight
to show me how you feel

Why is it Mother, that your eyes
do not light up with joy
when I come near to visit you
why is it Mother? Why?

You are polite, you greet me well,
you offer food and drink
you ask politely how I am
but oh, how I do wish

you'd smile at me so gleefully
and tell me that you missed me
and that I am the favorite one
among your pretty children.

I wish that you could recognize
that I have much to offer
oh, tell me that you're proud of me
and what I have accomplished.

Just let me hear you saying once
that you delight in me
and all that I have made of life,
my family, and me.

But no such joys will come to me
forever I shall miss them
you could not give what you don't have
perhaps you also missed them.

Haiku

Pale moon, setting sun
mottled green the rolling hills
kingbirds man teasel

Dusty lonesome road
summer meadow hosting deer
quail stir in the brush

Wheat field dry and hot
breezy cool the locust grove
magpies claim tree top

Deep blue sky, still air
meadowlark rises, spilling
song over meadow

Sun flickers on brook
berries glisten on the vine
hiding by the pool

Nis Randers - by Otto Ernst
translated by Rita Traut Kabeto

Crashing and howling and bursting night
Darkness aflame with furious might
A cry through the breakers.

The sky is on fire and it's clear as day
On the sandbank a shipwreck, still rocked by the waves
But gyres are pulling.

Nis Randers has seen, and calmly he says,
"One man is left clinging, out there, on the mast,
We'll get him, we must."

And gripping his arm, his mother says, "No!
You're all I have left, I can't let you go.
I will it, your mother.

"Your father was drowned, and Momme, my son;
and Uwe is missing these three years passed.
My Uwe, your brother."

With foot on the bridge, his mother in back,
He points to the wreck, and calmly he says,
"And his mother?"

He readies the boat, takes with him six more,
Great, hardy sons of Friesland's shore.
How the oars are flying!

Boat up and boat down, what a hellish dance.
It's bursting to pieces! No – not yet.
How long will it hold?

With fiery whips the ocean does lash
The man-eating horses, this way and that.
They're foaming and raging.

Their panting speed has coupled them tight
They rear and crowd each other with might
With hooves that are thrashing.

Three storms at once! They torch the world.
What's that? A boat! It's headed for shore!
They made it! They're coming!

And eyes and ears are straining to know
Quiet! A call! And then, once more:
"Tell Mother, it's Uwe!"

Nis was a Frisian, a member of a Germanic tribe that lived
along the Northern coast of Holland, roughly between the rivers
Rhein in the West and Ems in the East. They had their own
culture and language, but not much of it is left now.

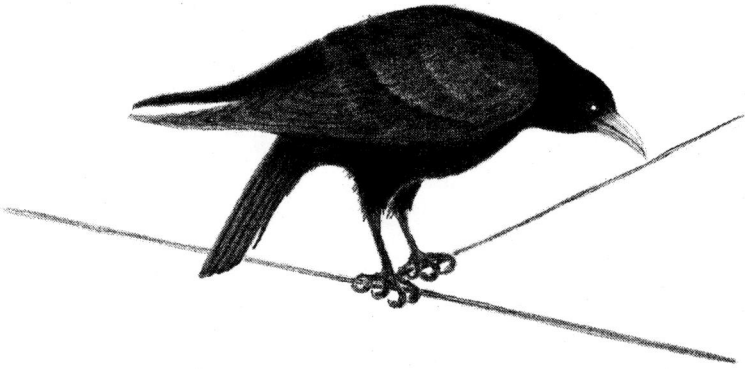

Crows in Summer

Some crow birds clung to a longish wire,
A heavily thick one for telephonire,
Crow number one was picking so deft
On a bone in his claw, acquired by theft.

He picked at the bone so heartily
That crow number two felt jealousy
And loudly demanded, "you selfish one, you
Save some for me, I am hungry too."

But Crow number one turned away from her
Continued to pick, could not be deterred
And grunted with mouth full of food half chewed,
"there's not enough meat on this bone for two."

Crow number two did scold and whine
In vain she was seeking a friendly invite
But all of a sudden, the bone did drop
To the sidewalk below with a loudish plop.

Crow number one then anxiously flew
Down to the sidewalk his bone to rescue.
He failed to notice a car shooting fore
From the neighboring house's garage door

The crow was careless, saw only the bone
The driver saw neither, ran over them both.
But crow number two hurried down real quick
delighted herself with a crow picnic.

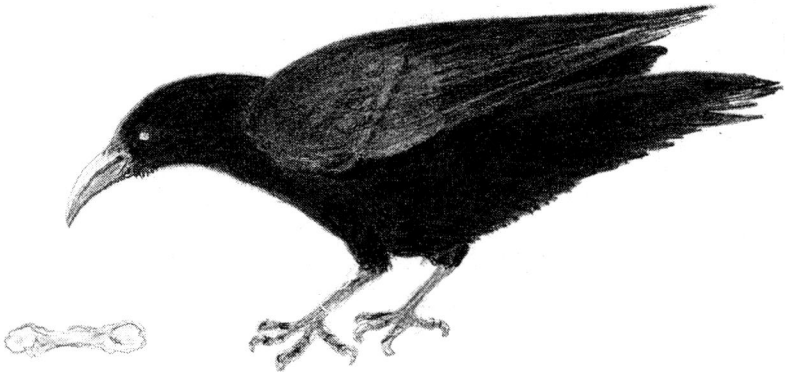

Haiku

Quiet pond, trilling
glossy black wing, red red patch
flutter in the reeds

Golden bristly wheat
lazy circling hawk shadows
harried fleeting mouse

Black cloud rags hurtle
blue and black the mountain ridge
startled killdeer wails

Marbled sunset sky
bluegrass sways gently, rocking
tiny butterflies

Blue Mountain Water

Among the rolling hills that hide
from city view and noise
that tiny precious wilderness
where Mill Creek fills the void

there, meadows roam the sun-drenched slopes
and blackbirds crowd the reeds
and sun-baked paths meander still
where wheat and locusts meet
and wildly thick the brambles grow
to dress the flood plain mud
and cottonwoods that drench in spring
the wilderness with fluff.

And housed is there what seeks to hide
well guarded what needs rest
and promise given of the same
to each and every guest.

Streamscape

Oh, to seek out the path of that winding stream
where it calmly yields to the rolling sea
on the sandy flats of the ocean shore
whence out of the rock strewn gully it tore
after fording a valley of sun-drenched pine
mullein, lupine, and columbine -

to answer the call of that beckoning stream
onward and upward to cool ravines
shaded by oaks and crowded with ferns
unrolling their leaves from the fragrant earth
where brambles are warp and vines the weft
that weave a dense blanket cross hollows and clefts -

to heed the tease of that zig-zagging stream
where it narrows and deepens with slowing speed
and wanting to rest the stream fills a gorge
of straight rocky walls lacking banks and ford
but throwing their shadows across the tarn
to paint the still water mysterious and dark –

to find the bubbly youth of that stream
as it wells up with vigor so fresh and clean
like children of man born of the Earth
belonging to all quite self unaware
washing 'round boulders and plowing through meadows
carving and shaping the land to its purpose.

But the highway sequesters that free-flowing water,
fences mark parcels and plats at its shoulders
bridges avoid it, I cannot get near
some roads run past but no chance to veer
from the byways of limits and traffic controls.
Life's gift of the streamscape is privately owned.

The Blue Mountains
in September

When the rain stopped the sun stood in the West.
As with a sudden impulse to lavish indulgence,
sunshine flooded the Eastern mountains
with an unearthly light
that flaunted a vast patchwork
of fields and gullies, trees and boulders,
pine woods and meadows and pinnacles
in the varied and muted greens and golds
of a dry hot summer
and framed it all with a perfect rainbow.

The Clearing

I didn't know what I would seek
when on a summer's day
a grove of firs I sought to join
't was waiting just for me.
Their branches meshed like holding hands
pretended firm resistance,
their fingertips of springtime green
once soft had grown quite prickly.

And summer's heat had roused the scent
of flowers, pine, and earth
so thick it seemed to linger on
the quivers in the air.
I pushed into that grove of trees
they parted willingly
and found a pristine clearing there
't was waiting just for me.

No shadow marred the sun-drenched scene
that spread before my eyes
and nothing stirred the drowsiness
played up by butterflies
and insects on their lazy rounds
of stately columbines,
and wispy grasses, sturdy mullein
and daisies snowy white.

I lay me down into that meadow
and closed my eyes to gaze
what eyes and ears can not perceive
for being jailed by brain.
So silently I lay and waited
as if I hoped to melt
into the one and other life
by heart alone beheld.

I hoped yet knew not who or what
was waiting there for me
my senses strained to take in what?
my restlessness increased.
And when I left that secret place
had promised me so much
a sigh wrung lose from deep inside
and tears rose in my eyes.

The Sound of Silence

The robin crowns the eve's demise
with song upon the silence
spilled like pearls across a canvas
of fiery red horizon.

Then frogs fall in with croaking
while crickets add their chirping
and pheasants sound the evening call
come blackbirds' final trillings.

And ere the moon has risen full
the coyotes start their howling
while geese are settling down with whoosh
of breaking feet on water.

But time has come for me to leave
this wondrous sounding silence
which echoes in my heart and mind
forever charm and solace.

The Story of the Tomatoes

Two gardens lay dreaming in sunshine bright
Owned by two sisters, called Distrust and Spite.
They grew many kinds of tree fruits and shrubs
Apples and berries, and all types of crops.

Each one of the sisters her garden did tend
With hope and ambition her plants defend'
'gainst bugs and disease; and bided the time
while tiny tomato plants grew to great height

And hung full of fruit, so red and so plump
So lovely to look at, so tempting to pluck
And promised the sisters delectable palate
They loved best of all the tomatoes in salad.

But then, one day, oh sorrowful truth
When Spite sought her garden to pick the fruit
What she did seek, so round and so ripe
Had vanished, was gone, was stolen at night.

"Who stole my tomatoes?" she said with wrath
while searching the ground for tracks of the rat
and noticed a shoe print embedded in dust
it came from the garden of sister Distrust.

Why did she do that, Spite wondered aside,
Has lots of her own, why rob me of mine.
And called to her sister when seeing her next
"did you like the stolen tomatoes, my Pet?"

"Yes, tell me," called sister Distrust in reply,
"why did you steal my tomatoes last night?
I know very well, you stole them from me
And now you dare to place blame on me."

Then Spite called back, "I saw proof of your deed,
your footprints, they pointed from you here to me."
Distrust got angry, "how dare you spread lies,
Your footprints, not mine, are proof of the crime."

"Your greed got you steeling tomatoes from me,
you cannot deny it!" the sisters did scream.
"You common thief," "you darn old fool,
don't need you stupid tomatoes for stew."

In the shade of the fruit trees a shadow sneaked off,
the thief of tomatoes, he grimaced and scoffed
For the theft, the evil, which he had committed
Now doubly afflicting the sisters has splitted.

The Old Apple Tree

My garden owns an apple tree
An ancient one, still growing keen
Way up above my gutter line
Despite of winter, wind, and ice.

The tree is twisted, gnarled and torn
Has lumps and bumps and scars galore
And where the trunk does leave the ground
a gaping hole a look allows.

The tree was hollowed long ago
No flesh remains, the bark does coat
An empty shell. Yet stood it strong,
Did never yield to winter's storm.

And every spring it blooms anew
And keeps its promise faithfully
Then drops in fall the ripened fruit
Like blessing on my house's roof.

Robots

three-armed robots
atop the bluffs
along the river
beside the road
amid the farms

towering high
above the crops
above the people
amid the cattle
and working hard

turning slowly
this way, that
changing bearing
as they must
to catch the wind

making power
ancients knew
was lately lost
recalled anew
by modern need

All Life is One

It is not good to be alone
Said God who knew it all
He said it to himself and then
To Adam passed it on.

And Adam understood and shared
This knowledge with his kin
And they in turn re-lived this truth
For those who followed them.

But somewhere there, along the time
The message got corrupted
And rugged individualism
Became what people covet.

Go West young man, the call went out
To several generations
Who left behind what tied them down
To people, land, and culture.

And on they moved from place to place
They never settled long
The ties grew thinner then, and weak
And one day they were gone.

But lacking ties we flounder like
A ship atoss at sea,
Like kite adrift on willful wind
For lack of solid string.

For where's no asking there's no answer
No intimate exchange
Of thoughts and feelings, minds and hearts
No kinship to be made.

No conversation to be nurtured
No time to ponder life,
Forgotten that our life's for living
Not chasing after price.

It is not good to be alone
Said God who knew it all
Yet lonely, God, we have become
Amid the largest throng.

Yet deep inside a silent place
We'll find again our way
To where we come from, who we are
And loneliness will wane

Life as Sparrow

If I could live like sparrows do
I'd be so very merry
Could be and do as I see fit
And never cause me worry

I'd build my nest without regard
to quality and price
With what's attainable and real
Regardless of the sight.

I would not care 'bout smog and din
For high above the dirt
I'd sing my song, my call, my tease
And never stop my flirt.

As sparrow I would never feel
lonely, sad, or fervent
Although, I fear that I would miss
The joy of love's endearment.

By the Light of the Moon

In a certain part of Germany, the official beginning of the Fasching season [the weeks before lent; it ends with Ash Wednesday] is November 11, at 11:11 a.m. A group of people who are associated with this event spend the Eve of that Day with a hike to the top of a prominent hill. A religious observance in a chapel built into the rock is followed by supper and social gathering in the nearby cabin. Although shut down for the winter, it is re-opened for this occasion.

On the Eve of Fasching season,
On a dark November night,
Hardy people, bearing torches
Climbed a mountain path

To usher in with humble prayer
The coming merriment
A little chapel set in rock
Made solemn the event.

A nearby cabin's fire, later
Gave comfort at the table
To friends and lovers, all belonging
Except for one among them.

Chatter, laughter, secret glances
Roused a jolly mood,
And the treasured songs of childhood
Filled the cozy room.

Laughter, chatter, songs, and glances
Swirled around the loner,
Numbed his senses like the whirling
Of a gay carousel.

And the whirling merriment
Distilled a thoughtful vein
He knew himself outside the group
He watched as through a veil.

Then suddenly, he left that room
To seek the lonesome night
With star and moonlight shining on
He reached the rocky height.

A lusty wind roared powerful
And scattered clouds like rags,
And tore at treetops, whipped the brush
And tousled distant flares.

It tugged and yanked at the intruder
It rummaged through his hair
It pushed and shoved him from behind
Was right into his face

Yet blissful smile the loner had
Like waiting for the wind
To pluck him off the mountaintop
And take him on its wing.

And turning to the moon, he bathed
His face in mellow light
As if he hoped it would reveal
The wisdom from on High.

An offering, he stood and merged
Into the wild embrace
Of wind and moon and mountain top
At one in hallowed space.

The Route-and-Rally Way
of Civilization

Our western culture did not move
At straight and steady forward pace
it moved from lows to highs and lows
again, the route-and-rally way.

It could not grow from then to now
In rigid, straight and narrow path
For mankind's actions have affects
On what is now and comes to pass.

A culture starts, it lives and grows
It blossoms keenly, then it goes
And joins the ranks of glories past
Will not return as once it was.

Then follow certain times of darkness
When inner forces work and drive
To bring about a new momentum
That sprouts and feeds renewed life.

And if you think that our cherished
State of the union cannot perish
Then watch and heed what it uncovers,
This route-and-rally way of eons.

If Presidents Wore Knickerbockers
and governors did the like,
then bankers, mayors, senators, too
would gladly fall in line.

The Judges in their longish robes
That hide the real man
may well be wearing them right now,
It's really hard to tell.

If men wore knickerbockers then
There'd be no need for ties,
That noose would look ridiculous
With knickerbocker style.

Without the tie, the men would feel
Much freer, less controlled,
And that would lead to longer lives
And happiness of soul.

Then premiums for life and health
Insurance would come down
It means more money then for fun
Less stress the men to hound.

If presidents wore knickerbockers
Then women could do too
And wear whatever feels right good
No need to put on suits.

Without the strangling pantyhose,
That bane of female lives,
There'd be no need for pencil heels
The bane of feet and spine.

They wouldn't yell at children then
At husbands, colleagues, peers,
They'd have the patience of old Job
Less stress and much more cheer.

And all that joy and ease would come
To be our well-trod path
If only we could get the Pres'
To wear those great old pants.

Smart Crow

I saw a crow come swooping down,
A piece of bread it carried 'round,
It settled on my bird bath rim
To quench its thirst by dipping in
Its beak which held the dry old crust
That fell into the water, drat!

But undismayed the crow did drink
The water from my bird bath sink
And quenched its thirst, then took what was
The dry old crust now turned to mush
And gulped it down right easily
I do believe, quite knowingly.

Six Sisters

I have six sisters, heaven knows
I never asked for them
It's Father's fault who longed for boys
yet Mom birthed only femmes.

My sisters roam my head and heart
I did not give them right
Quite unabashedly they make
An impress on my life.

The one does hardly speak at all
So I must always ask,
The other sister never stops
I wish that she'd shut up.

Another one gave me offense,
Perhaps it was a jest,
The eldest one has lectured me
But does not give her best.

My youngest sis, the snippy one,
Tells me the facts of live,
And therefore thinks herself more smart
Than all of us combined.

The second one is so suspicious
She does not take my word
For anything I say, she does
Misunderstand the world.

Number three is lacking humor
Five is missing tact
And one has answers ready made
Before she hears what's said.

Now far from home and lonely oft,
I'm thinking of my treasures
and long to spend my life among
my six beloved sisters.

Sun
radiant light
diffused in sky
flooding our days
with ethereal rays
reflected in ocean
continuous motion
spreading the glimmer
and deepen the shimmer
increasing the shine and
returning the light
to radiant
Sun

The Blue Mountains
in February

The setting sun flooded the Western sky with liquid gold,
tinting cloud ripples that turned pink
as they fanned out from North to South.
In the East, the snow-covered mountain range faded slowly
into a cold and grayish haze that rose from the foothills.
It thickened and darkened and rose higher
until the tree-lined silhouette vanished
in awesome loneliness and silence.

Stoking the Fire

I do not belong to a family
of closely knit individuals,
but rather, I'm part of an entity
that clings to precarious unity
like a fire about to go out.

Six sisters and I and our only brother
steadily attempt to love one another
for previous generations' incessant feuding,
fighting and spying and hatred breeding
had put out the fire of love.

But my sisters and I and our only brother
try very hard to get along with each other
and rally staunchly in Mother's place
to celebrate special and ordinary days,
feeding and stoking that fire.

How sweet it is after years of absence
when ruffled feathers had time to settle,
tempers have mellowed, insults forgotten,
and time makes precious events of the moment -
to feel that fire of love

on a cold and miserable winter day
as I come through the door that's broad and plain
and look on my sisters and only brother
crowding the entry around our mother -
how it flares, that fire of love

in the cozy comfort of the entry way
that's filled with memories of kids at play
we spend the first hugs and kisses around,
carefree reviving and making devout,
renewing that fire of love.

Epilogue

I cannot claim to have created
the words and verse I write
since evermore they have existed
throughout this thing called time.

That seamless boundless time contains
all future, present, past
it holds whatever was and is
and what not yet has passed.

And all that is required then
is pondering in silence
to come upon the words and verse
awaiting in abeyance.

Like mist or vapor they surround me
and occupy my space,
quite fully structured they await
their passage through my brain.

They come to me when Self is free
of self and worldly din
like Spirit's voice that I can hear
in secret whisperings.

The words and verse I love to write
appeared when I could trust
that time would yield its treasures when
my self had given up.

Content

A Daughter's Plea...................................29
A Prayer..23
All Life is One......................................47
Ants..6
Ash Wednesday.....................................17
Blue Mountain Water.............................37
Blue Mountains in February.....................59
Blue Mountains in September...................39
By The Light of the Moon.......................50
Childish Quest.......................................28
Clearing, The.. 40
Crows in Summer..................................35
Crows in Winter....................................14
Daisies..16
Epilogue..61
Haiku...31, 36
Hot Crow..5
I Can Not Go to Work Today....................12
If Presidents Wore Knickerbockers.............53
Intermezzo..19
Life as Sparrow....................................49
Love's Issue..3
Mums..27
Nis Randers..32
Old Apple Tree, The...............................45
Robots...46
Route-And-Rally Way of Civilization.............52
Sidewalk...11
Six Sisters..56
Smart Crow...55
Sound of Silence, The.............................42

Stoking the Fire……………………...…………60
Story of the Tomatoes, The………………………43
Streamscape………………………………....…38
Sun……………………………………………58
To Robert Frost on 'Mending Walls'……………... 8
To Robert Frost on 'Stopping by Woods'……...…2
Unsecured Places……………………………...…20
Village Lane, The………………………….....25
Vine, The……………………………………….1
What Then?……………………………….....10
White Man……………………………………...…7